RAVEN EYE

Volume 60

Sun Tracks
An American Indian Literary Series

Series Editor
Ofelia Zepeda

RAVEN EYE

Poems by Margo Tamez

The University of Arizona Press

Tucson

The University of Arizona Press
© 2007 by Margo Tamez

Library of Congress Cataloging-in-Publication Data
Tamez, Margo.
    Raven eye : poems / by Margo Tamez.
        p. cm.— (Sun tracks ; v. 60)
    ISBN-13: 978-0-8165-2565-2 (pbk. : alk. paper)
    ISBN-10: 0-8165-2565-X (pbk. : alk. paper)
    I. Title.
PS3570.A446R38 2007
811'.6—dc22   2006025488

Publication of this book is made possible in part by
the proceeds of a permanent endowment created with
the assistance of a Challenge Grant from the National
Endowment for the Humanities, a federal agency.

Manufactured in the United States of America on acid-
free, archival-quality paper.

12 11 10 09 08 07   6 5 4 3 2 1

FOR MY CHILDREN

Contents

This Medicine

Acknowledgments

Gratefulness

To the ancestors. To Hawk, Milpa, Maura, Aria. To Justin. To Erik, you came to the field of war with pure-light love and carried us on your back to refuge, where we could be human . . . thank you for living through the obsessions.—M.T.

——

The following poems were published or will be published in the following publications in the same or modified forms.

American Poetry Review: "She Wakes Up to Watch the Sky" [previously published as "Corazon Wakes Up to Watch the Sky"] (1997), "The Digging Hole," "What She Knows," "Playing Hangman" (2005)

Flyway: A Literary Review: "Whipping Pole" ["A Reasonable Silence"]

Hawaii Pacific Review: "El Dorado, Inc." ["This Twisted Storm of Wind," "Where We All Begin," "Hanging from Red Cord"]

Hayden's Ferry Review: "Ceremony of Peyote"

Naked Wanting: "Smooth Pink Blossoms"

RAVEN EYE

Who will return lamps to the smelted sky?
Who will remember the knots that held up sun?

O! sky!
O! luminous tree!
O! raven! O! muted one!

Falling water
Falling down
Croaking raven
Flutter wind
Nobody hears
not the sound
nor the thought

O! fist!
O! fist on raven's head!
Is it night's or is it sun's?
Or is it the war?
Or the world of wars?

Stranger moon
Stranger moon
Strange on the moon

O! raven! O! flutter!
O! leaves! O! falling!

Wings and body snagged
On barbed wire
Technology of war

O! periphery!
O! humans!

Broken wing
Spitting gravel

Denting the metal
Armor of sky

The Rattle of Bones for Hours

She Wakes Up to Watch the Sky

At night on the rez no lights
No lights at night   no electric
At night   no running water   no plumbing
Nothing wet   but me at night I piss outside
Under stars   they're brighter   on the rez
At night   sometimes I see   waves auras UFOs
Under the stars   all the witnesses die in darkness
When they die at night and I'm finished pissing
I stand   under stars
Standing naked last night I saw this star
Fast fast it went   from east to west
From east to west this fast light went
Ghoul   alien   ancestor   fool
A fast witness   flies the sky
Spits and cackles
Splits silver shimmer   at night   I pray to
Lady of Dissent a silverblack thrashing whirl
Screechcalls blast her membrane   birthing
A blackfeather body   flails his wingbones crack
The dry encrusted back of Gila River
Collides   into   the rock cavern eye
Of M Mountain   elders still call
Holy place   where Moctezuma's   pocked spiritbody
Returned home

Sex Blood

Together the first time lying on the knoll
The slope of hill and buffalo grass
Strain in our bodies   against all the
Tremulous prisms on the face of pond

My first blood spreading through my girlfriend's
Best dancing dress   a chintz of irises and poppies

I am thinking this isn't any good—
A man plunging my darkness *o you're so tight*   metalnight
His full thrust into me   like I'm a void   feared edge
A map he'll fall off of   fall into chasm chaos madness
Feels like hanging upside down   the same way
I hung upside down from a thick tree branch
When I was a girl poor mixed-race   violence and surveillance
A.m. to   p.m.
Rushed into my hips
The fast rush   the fast knowing   the fast thrust
That only   deciding   to fall from the branch
Will stop

Swallowing humidity each time
I opened   him shoving himself further inside
Was slow twists   jabs   shudders
Straining against his chest   shoving him off

Not knowing if the nothing existed
Beyond this swallowing noise of the body
The throat I might become
Something else exposed for the predator
In gunmetal light of the waxing moon

This Twisted Storm of Wind

I thought I smelled a strange smoke
But it was me   burning
A bundle of sage   traded in Montana
Another lifetime ago   near a town   Philipsburg
Where townspeople stamp down stamp down stamp down
12,000 years of encampments   bison   flint   turquoise

Smoking

Where a history of naming
Privileges the takers

Stamping out breath

Dozens of flies think
Like twisted storms of wind

I know a man with a head and a voice
Like prickly desert weeds
Foxtails in autumn

Said he owns my contours
The rocky boundaries I know

I tell him he makes crude sounds
Insulting creeks leaves and passages

Inside me   divots and stones
Laying hidden beneath loam

Still   I went headfirst
Into this storm

After colliding, Raven recalls: Where We All Begin

I am the sex between thorns   scent
And a pulse
Dwelling in the lips of captured   raped   indentured
Lipan slaves   Spanish peasants   Jumano refugees

Fertility   possibilities   questions   entrapment
Spawn this memory like an instruction book:
hate them   hate yourself   turn the screw tighter   repeat

My wings come back . . . one . . . two
To a wet slippery cry   of bone and memory   retrieval

Where the universe begins
Where the universe begins   where the universe begins

Where we all begin

Ceremony of Peyote

A snakebird   sinuous dim form   silhouetted
On the porchroof of the hogan—

Comes out of a monsoon sky
Banded thickly   red and flint

Snakebird in me   curves slowly
Over my bed

The sinew of what can't be said

Nine months full of ocean and yolk
Scents of beautifully made starmatter

A smell of tongue and lip
Of moisture a scent of Snaketown's Gila clay

I'm a brown and black puddle   a scent I know

—————

You spent hours in the heat of midday   fidgeting with rage
I'm unpredictable   not the kind of Indian   you can present   to

Men all wrapped up behind panIndian shawls   eagle fans
Who never bring their women to pray
Whose diabetic eyes devour
My pregnant belly
Full of a bird boy   raven boy
Ripe with beautiful worlds

Corn meat and berries
You say the order
Morning food for the relatives   *always like that*   you say
The look in your eyes   *don't mess up*   *don't embarrass me*
   don't talk too long when you pray for the water

Can't risk my prayers to the morning star
Risk what I can say about
This medicine a Mexican Indian woman brought
North   got Christianized   by subjugated men

My morning prayers only suitable
For waterbirds
Anhingas and herons
Not men or women
In shawls
Fanning and chanting
In chorus of what they deny

My body
The yolks of my body
Stories we must tell to undo
What has been done

Bird Boy of the Blue Light
for H

These moments exist like light
Fades from a gas lantern
The way mantles wilt into sacs
Like thin flesh

Your brown fingers   rounded tubular
Can only be searching for more breast
Tiny nails pinching and clutching in for milk

———

You're on a frail passage

Absorbed into my body like loam

———

I see two choices here

The foreground—
Ironwood autumn corn amaranth   roan shadows   everything
I've denied

Beyond that the blurred hue of dark

Like a shape I've recognized
But neither shunned
Nor welcomed

———

Your soul is water
And blue light
Sparking flashes all around you
In this dark space

———

Me inside you

———

You show me your hands
Signing

Stop them

I'm falling

Catch   me
I'm crashing   mother   mother

———

You are like a rare dark moss
From a secret cavern
Abruptly unearthed in a quake

Clinging to crumbled rocks

Which suddenly stop moving
Revealing clouds   dust   debris

An Inca dove
Impaled by thorns of a fallen saguaro
She struggles to stay alive

Her frantic flapping of wings
Quashed into silence

Playing Hangman

Were those sounds you heard tumbling in womb water
The sweaty fright when nightmare people
Snatched you
Battering you the way dream people do
As if we should expect it
As if we should've known better

But we're afraid so afraid to budge or do anything about
Anything   fear of retribution
As we grasp the blanket tighter   binding our hands
Clutched into fists

———

He put a hold on me in a boozed daze
The sweat catching glints of dawn light
Trapped like a captive spirit inside the bead
Dripping at the end of his nose   sweat
Freckling his skin like a pocked disease
The worn sheet he pressed across my face   stifling
To breathe

Over and over the bitching   like at so many wakes
The droning sound of chants   cranky out-of-tune guitars
Played by exhausted Indian women
Singing gospel songs   always hopeful you'll like them
How they play
Tell them they're good and   you feel close to the one
Who died   everyone   so hungry   to be witnessed

But mostly you know that the ones bitching
Over the donuts and Hawaiian punch
Are the ones like the one holding the sheet over your face
Who have the most collusion with daily casualties
The ones prattling on about rescuing mother earth are the
Least tolerant
Of Indian women and real revolution

It's all right alright already
That's enough!
Stop!

I'll never stop

━━━

Your sigh says fleshy threads and venous lining
Stretched   then wove   red-blue muscles
Satiny cords lifted your birth sac
And the warm gold sea fed you

Your life was lovely then

There's the tornado in your throat   blowing
The trailer off its pillars
My voice   cracking   above the engine-roar of green air
Rocking surge
Blood flow   a heated contraction   muscles above your head
Your voice

Mimics my rise   the train-scream of wind   shatter
Broken glass
Screams of his other woman's children   fed on her been-
Done-wrong rage
Whimpering with the dark held closely   only that time
To my mammoth stomach   the leaking breasts

M Mountain

at the Gila River Crossing

I turn off the pavement onto a dirt road   where
Men from the rez collect firewood
And love being chased by the tribal cops
Bored   and even   more bored
Laughing their asses off   the adrenaline of being chased

Hundreds of prayers fly out of me   fly out
My truck speeding across desert
Braking here every time   like bright flares
Signaling   *seeeeeeee meeeeeee*

How many others' prayers at this colossal fractal stone
Attempt to divine the convergences—   longing
Irritation   denial
And the fringes from where we dare   to be
More   than survivors

Famished eyes and craving mouths of other pilgrims
Who crawled up the mountain before me
Leave   no clues   behind

The usual silence says   *figure it out woman*

Fragile leaves falling off
A mesquite branch in winter
Jumping cholla long dried and brittle
Nerve like a shriveled curled thumb
Sun and moon like monks in hermitage
Water scarcely trickling to springs beneath

Inside out outside in of what doesn't stand up
To chance   to risk

A lashed animal on a chain straining to utter
The hesitant
Naked words then   no sound   when habit
Shoves the moment
Where no one can get away   where no one
Knows   how

His rough rush towards quick sex
Straining beneath the force   my cervix
Cramping
A violent release   usual hatred   then no
Sound

No   sound   No sound

No sound

The Birth of Thought Woman

Children shrink from blood
Relations whose faces dictate them   *trust*
Whose hands and words peck
The order   like sport

Relatives say
Maize saves people from themselves

This food is medicine
Says the road man

But the medicine is laced   uranium   rape   DDT   lynching
Toxaphene   apartheid   radiation   blood violence
And the seed keeper rapes his wife like
Pistons ram inside pipes
And his sons rape her daughter like
Scissors want to cut
Smash her son's head   as tidal waves
Pound the shore

We didn't count on that but were warned and English says
Little in long sounds with no air
The fetus inside the moon curdles in her
Milkysoft placenta   we're going back in
Time to the end of the barbed world
English says
Little in long sounds
No air
I tell the rapist's words to my grandmothers
To my grandmothers   to my grandmothers

Splitting my body

Making me unnatural

When I walk away from
The shove of wounds

I am sound before language
Before language
Before all language until
Spider's web spins and unfurls her next move

Thought . . . it's your turn to be born
War is at hand

Hanging from Red Cord

There exists
A hand-carved boat
With a way to go
Up the long length
Of river
Clogged
By invasive species
Toxic sludge

The river calls
In any case
Contaminated or not

Calls a song   moony waxing waft
Heart of a silverhair
Grandma calling with instructions

Outfitted with a bone knife
Pounding stone
Dried nuts   wolfberries   mesquite   nopales
Drinking water and wool blankets woven and dyed the old way

I close my eyes
Grasp my knife
Hanging from red cord
Around my neck   a gift
From she who emerged from water slicklove   wet
Pressing her motherlove into me

Practice
Knowing the beast
Do
What is necessary
She chanted

Addiction to the Dead

I lift my body one leg then another over the cold curve of
the claw-foot tub
Like a walking stick with a colossal cocoon attached
A beast and a mutant   I am this

Hooked on the steam of hot water I
Negotiate stretched skin   a sore spine   the splitting of imminent birth

What do you want

Mammoth   a domemoon stomach
Carved by spidery trails   former settlement

You in there   *baby*   think you're ready for this

Sing soprano notes   sing sounds of upness
Says the midwife
She says *go ahead   smoke some marijuana* you see she's our
*motherherb   sacred medicine   not for foolery and
selfishness   never to be used in that other way you know
she works deeply niece   can take care those injuries
bad mister   wrecks   he set   snaring you
this medicine will   show you   the things killing
all of us*

——

This is what's necessary   I sustain you
You are not ready for me   what is out here

Cruel minds separate small girls from girlhood
Fists pound your brother's brains through the wall
Yellowdrunk eyes from a failed mind   lick every pair of
Breasts in the room
At home the smoke shop the wake the burial the ceremony the
Indian-taco stand—

I'm done

━━━

Just keep sleeping on my mucous pillow
And don't push on me

O   pouring bowls of light
I see the horrific truths
The most beautiful lie
Will never fool

Never fool
Never fool
The fool

━━━

What will be the venting of this
Where will we be
How will the vault be lifted

A tinny sound   the drip of persistence
Water into water looking for its level
Always seeking level

No more a drip now a stream continuous motion
Unified atoms
Pearls cells threads cries

The house and early night are each black and black

One a lonesome gaping mouth   the other a safe place
To plan
The real fact of spirit leaving body

———

You push to be born fully alive
You press my addiction to the dead world
Birth me out a muse

———

Ancestors glide
Landing on the levee where DDT petroleum and tobacco
Burned my grandfather's flesh *Emiliano*   and fueled
My mother's resistance *Chata*

Ancestors scold me   the lanky child running through
Glossy fields
Crabgrass Indian gum plants johnsongrass

Waxy from spraying   the continuous spraying
O freedom of the green revolution   O postwar
Stockpiles

O   fucking   inheritance   of the ethnic poor

O   how   we've   been   fucked

———

I go through the window opening after opening
Memory buried upon memory   that's how this appears

Skins   burst   unseam   and inside these is me
A skinny dark girl with a dark brain and a dark mind

Seeking the deja-vu   Zone of Time Flow
Outside of fear

O   no one   can see me   or see what is real
The invasive spray seeping
Follows me and flows in my blood through decades

To my room and the ease of dark and sleep
Dreaming how I'll wage war on my raiders

O settlers of the empire
O land thieves
O scalpers of my grandfathers
O slave traders of my grandmothers

Books   stand like enemies
Rapists   who'll conspire to kill me

They wrestle me   I wrestle back   kicking their spines
Splitting their black seeds with my knife   the little
Black letters ejaculate from
Their splintered and crushed chaff

My uterus stops   the surging jolt of *you*   kicking
You will not miscarry
Not one more
Not ever again

Corn Girl Dawn Girl

Sun rising   sun rising
Corn Girl's humming
O! Ga'an! O! white shell!
O! ancestors!

Playing her wooden flute
A spirit of rescue in her small hands
Her lungs   her breath

She doesn't see boogeyman

Her memory of rape
Down beneath soil level
Deep in the vague shadows
Of infancy

I don't . . . Can't . . .
Run away . . . just run
You have to get safe
O god   o god

Here mama   it's ok   listen to the sounds
You are here you are here you are here

Whipping Pole

Do we know how we come to a reasonable silence

Monsoons and inevitability storm in
Riding on slanted wind   thin flat sheets   dark steel
Santana's *what you need is what you want* belting out
Broken windows   glass knives hanging
On strings of caulking
Clink-clinking   and a doorway forced wider
Impaled by a split plank

Hail marks small o's onto the floodplain
A lake   of little mouths
And wind shoving them away

What you need is what you want
What you need is what you waaaaaaaannnt

A mojave's storm song a mojave's poison inking the sky
In diamond scales birthing thousandheaded serpents
And one luminous snake grins coming awake
Her fluttering colors blend fractal stones   volcanoes
Hillsides   dreams songs desire wreck my antiquity

What fills this void from   past voids

We don't always   get   to   know

The hands of the storm enclose   re-shaping the
Dissonance and dissent between belting rain and rage
Gathering them both in his wretched palms   fisting

The two tightly
Like precious gambling stones   divining them
Rattling the magic bones   for hours

The porch post was an anchor   and a whipping pole

And there were only two choices—one was lame and whimpering

The other   to stand against the storm   don't hold on
Or believe anymore in   safety or rescue
Just take direct action

Rain lashing me snake throwing us wind
Shoving me against   myself
And   a slanted doorframe

———

When he drove here to find
Some twisted way back into the worst choice
After the decade's and rez's   worst storm   mud flying
And his face ash-bare   visible   between
Four large hoops of mud
His truck tires spinning like blenders—
I'd been on the porch staring at

Stars beyond the flintjaw of sky
Standing from early   light to dusk
Leaning on the shovel   ready to strike   with
Everything to protect

He didn't ask about the sopping clothes   sucking my
Body's shape
Still ripe from recent birth   the baby perched
Next to a small fire   in a basket
I put together from fragments of a chair   chewed up
By a hungry wind
Nor about the evidence of force strewn over the land

Raven   Corn Girl

Whimpering splinters
In this new plateau where ocean   hundreds of miles and
Centuries away
Got sucked into desert's   scorched rectum

How the two children   their chaos of memory
Sneak a hiding space in the crevice
Between water and night
Sifting through eternal divisions   eruptions
Inhale the   first breath of dawn
Blue moons   disruption

Now the storm's ruin is merely a bog   panting
The fatigued breath   of an elder laborer
Grateful for rest

Which   was just another illusion
Another sky opened   and something else
Was coming this way

The Unpredictable Shoves

Corn Girl

Every living thing struggles
Pure and cutting
Like blazes and cross-hatched lines
In the forgotten shards of our lungs and our minds

Drought   heat   cold
The unpredictable   shoves of wind

Survival exposes you
To forces raging from the underside
Where peace is a foil

A voice comes to me in dreams
Sounding like flowers and pollen
Life and color   then I sleep
This is where deception
Kicks in

Close your eyes   this is how they seduce
Forget   part of the deception

The Breath Moves Corn Girl

A small thing   a gesture
Breaths taken slowly   filling capillaries
More blood circulating   actions to other actions

Becoming nothing
But a vague un-moment the fear having everything
To do with
What is always at stake

Back to breath—

In   all that is unforgotten
Out   all that is necessary

To go forward

I ask about expansion
As if I could
As if I had a right to

Her fingers ripple her breath out the flute

Breath
Forward again

Breath

Steady steady
Quick then slow

What do you remember
What do you cocoon
What memories will erupt
When you lie with your lover in the future
His penis or her fingers touching your vulva's moist lips
After you cringe from the force of
His dry cock or her fingernails
Scraping your delicate flesh

Will you remember this night
The scent of tortillas burning
Your half-brother
Using your infant body
His hands clasped around your small hips
Raking you up and down
Across his naked groin

Feel   the breath move you

To spaces of worlds   you feel   all around

No Time in This Storm

Pounding like fists against the breastbone
A stampede a tsunami   dust and storm clouds towering
In the short distance

Indecision
Has no time in this storm

Change

Its grip and strained knuckles
Tosses rooftops
Like a spree of acid-tripping demons

Exposing the vulva of expectancy   inside the houses
Quivering   waiting

The gales whip the ground   fences   milk goats

Who act as if huddling and ducking one's head
Under the other's udder
Is a forestalling against the storm's greed

The mind wants to believe and tries

What the mind wants to overcome is deception

The only thing that is there
Is the force   the exposed fear   and the expectancy

The Digging Hole

The femurs jangling from a mechanic's pulley
In the back field

And memory of men slaughtering spring pigs
Throwing beer cans to the ground
Joking about the potent liver
And looping coils of intestines
The curds of fat cells clinging deftly
To the thick heart

This morning the pumice-bones   brittle
Still hang by ropes   clattering underworld messages
Odd wind chimes rattle and chitter discontent

The night fills limply   pale clouds
Exhausted from rains
Meek implications of spent rage

Soon skies will spread their dank minds
As thin as grandma's old scarves

How water smells like more   than any of us ever were
In common

Tomorrow I'll see the stump of a dead cottonwood
Viewed and considered each morning
Near the road to town   on dark mornings
My headlights streak by fast
Like a well-aimed spear

The stump stares back at me

Its gnarled shape like a man hunched over
Repentant   his chin digging a hole through his chest
And his back twisted   ashamed and punished
For all his cruelty   for all he denies

Tomorrow's freedoms have no sleeves
Exposing skin to   air   heat   chemicals
The unwanted   malicious touch

Is the thread this weaves looping
Into a web

Sorrow! Sorrow!

The sun says with a sudden mouth
Dismissing my knowledge behind a stonesmooth cloud

Smoothed flat by the storm's palm

Where it was recently the fist ripping open sky

Ripping cervix   brisk   quick   wide

The ones huddling and waiting out the storm
Get flattened across the certainty of a coming front

The sun   drags their voices under
To the kiln

Resisting
They tilt their faces to the sky
As if it is the last jar of water

The word etched on the bottom

Change

Psychedelic

A pipe wrench hanging from a hole
Where a knob should be

Keeps the door and the trailer weighted down
Against winds panting at the door

The wooden door hanging slant on its hinges
Is not open

A sudden wind may push the baby
Right off the porch   head over feet

She won't be expecting to see a kaleidoscope

sky-door-porch-sky-door

To be knocked so completely onto a barrel cactus

Praise to thick cloth diapers

The pipe wrench stays tied to the door with a hole
Where the knob once was

The flies linger at the jamb

Their legs fixed to the trembling mesh screen
Signaling   another storm approaches

Their eyes glowing psychedelic

What Good Is a Chore

I draw lines

A spiral becomes an eye
An eyebrow becomes another fluid line
Becoming the nose and dark lip
Of a mouth that says
Eye have been better b4

The kitchen pulls its doorknobs clutching clothing
A preference for pockets when I walk by

Moving away from a finished chore
A quick *rip!*   of threads
Jerks me back and   I'm screwed to the nail

The discontented ugly rises   and says   *return return*
To toilet bowl chores

A quick *jerk*   back
Rips my sleeve on the nail holding a damp towel

Limp and frayed   applauding jeering
The snag of a good blouse

Need is the slave of want

What good is a chore done spitefully

An angry door

A resentful toilet

Drinking under the Moon She Goes Laughing:

When the end was near
He threatened   hands trembling
There is no end   never   his hands reaching to my face
You can't leave taking off his shirt going for his pants
The trickle of sweat beading off his nose

Moon-orb spray   metallic shimmer   slicklove
Tripping numb night shadows
Crows perched on a streetlight

We're terrestrial ants living in fragility
On Huhugam sacred ground
Jar of our dead

Like ragged cats my ghosts and I
Gossip in the alley behind a bar
My eyes grasp theirs   a spark   revolution
Feet without tracks on gravel

Our existence erased   far off
From clinking beer bottles and vanity

On the bench outside a bookstore
We get erased   see the news of the street
Resistance getting milled

My favorite ghosts and I bear down harder   birth ourselves

On the bench outside a bookstore
Frigid wind wants to snatch our secrets

Hey nay ya na ya na ya na
I thank you thank you for your presence
My ghosts I thank you for your presence
Hey nay ya na ya na ya na ya na
This dilemma oh ancestors
O! ancestors !!!! I thank you thank you thank you
Hey nay ya na ya na ya na ya na

I'm still the Lipan Jumano land-grant mongrel
Nobody sees nobody recognizes an invisibility
Scudding through all the checkpoints
Border towns train tracks pesticide flybys welfare lines

Wings shifting shape
Scorpion's venom injects me for the night

Green light spasms in the click click delete cut paste
fucking do something do something different

An orgasm of light at the slippery edge
One good time to die
And live spreading like osmosis

Tripping grandmother rabbit on the moon
Always with that sorrowful look on her face
Make the medicine
Be artistic
Do what is necessary

Smooth Pink Blossoms

We can't take back or clench in our throats this damage
Like replacing one cheap necklace for another

Our words run hard through certainty's only door
The guilty accused and forced into light

Not saying anything more
Before the fight
I unmask
On the lookout for new protections

My body and three sacred openings three sacred sisters
Smooth velvet   vulva pink and wrecked

My own and my children's bodies trumpet the horrific

Against the will of violation   I plant a garden
I take it all   infliction and bounty

We are not inherently violable
We are not inherently violable

Earth has no name for this   no name no name no name

My body
A smashed forest

Inside my womb
Flesh is storm skies

With my unborn dead buried   my bones broken   all I've become
Staring back at me
You! You! You!   All I've become   shrieking   a wind
Caught in between cracks of the doorjamb   and the door

I'm curling over for hard winds
Daily the wounds dry   and close
Smooth pink blossoms

I dance with dawn skirts   shell necklaces   cedar   sage
Tobacco
Chanting firehearth songs of all the brightness
I promise
I promise
I promise
I promise

From my perch above the elderberry
My aim separates   identifies   lets go my arrow

Into the beast on the bare forest floor

Make the medicine

Flesh Offerings

All the glass shivers
Though like glass is meant to break
Or rattle and scissors want to cut
The glass shatters the battle of wind
With the drama of all glass

Lightning changes the day
Into a new possibility
A mistaken identity
A gift without a name tag

Molecules and organisms
Come hurtling from the sea

Sneezes and hiccups
From dolphins and tilapia
Who swim where Cortés sailed
And lost

New stories
Get born in storms
Smelling like winter
And planets turning
At that precise second
And nothing can go back

Though going back still means
Change
Which is

Everything we ever need
And then can't possibly keep
Coveted beneath our jackets

A lover's mouth neglected
Without kisses or good chocolate
Not even warm cabernet
Becomes a cave of chattering stones

Stretched like bands down his face
And the change there
Would be
That eventually the lines
Like all rubber bands
Erode in deprived climates
And snap

Language   a snip and prick
Of flesh offerings

Desire converts to more potent needs
Saving myself from metal roof panels
Or the barbed wires
The storm flails them both

Tossing abuse freely
In each direction
Just duck or find cover

The photos flying in spirals
Above our heads

Are us
Before change and the storm
Came to wreck what we thought
Was already as far down as we could go

What we were
Is what we become

A chain of fear and hives
A super-real rope itching its chatter
Across my belly

The real head and real spine
Of a new child pressing on my cervix
Raises thumb to mouth
Salutes the storm and the wreckage
In her jellygold waters

This Medicine

Take This Medicine

Kisses and herbs
Clean the gash in Raven's scalp

His blood soaks a freshly washed cloth
Feast day cloth   Bread into body   Water into wine

Always-clean always-washing   Clothes or rags
Old things to be thrown out

━━━

She sees Raven   A whittled
Little boy

The horse of remorse   A throat without a croak

The ruse noose

A mute flute

━━━

Memory chews the corners of the table
Like kids teethe on chicken bones   Gnawing them smooth
The how of when everything ends
How everything pushes out the cervix

━━━

His face in the dirt
By two-by-fours

And rusty metal roofing
Harvested from white folks' alleys in Phoenix
And the reservation landfill

Raven remembers to remember
Each part
Remembering linked to a breath
Inside his body

Huddled over during beatings
Don't say anything

For words don't stop   this   from   that
Or that from this

To slow his heart   a   slight   murmur
Remembering to breathe

——

The stepbrother raped Corn Girl
Following her scent of vulva
To know himself

He shoved one finger two fingers then himself inside her

Raven knows
Raven breathes

——

In his mind where Raven is Super Apache Tough Guy
He'll always annihilate him
Jump him   rip him   off her   off himself

54

In his mind

———

He raped her   Raven knows

———

Raven the Mute
Muted muted boy
Mutating

———

No common raven   *Corvus corax*
Less the song   diminished
Confused with hawk or crow
Raven   nevertheless   never less
Less
And not visible   when in flight

Most excellent flier   in movies   in songs   in poems
Engaging in aerial acrobatics   at great heights
Where flight is an alternation of wing   flapping   gliding

Raven moves to a memory of an old song   slow wing beats
Before   the movies   before poems   before
But not here
Raising the slabweight off the grub night
Sloughing light   silted light   sifting dust   from his lips

———

The cursive *mine 4ever*   initialed by a knife
Catches salt   bread crumbs   occasionally egg yolk
Seasoning these fucking engraved curves which she curses
Picking them clean with the tine of a fork
Scrubbing down the salvaged oak for another meal

Kitchen tables are for everyone
Thus it seemed crude
To be reminded daily of being marked
Imagined as property   *4ever*

She glares at the thrift store buy
Four legs dry as femurs
Wobbling   but put to use

Never money to get better chairs
At Target in Tucson   or Wal-Mart in Casa Grande
Those thick cushions sewn into the seats

Just smelly thrift shops from a dirt town down highway 84
Factory-farmed cows
Rot and antibiotics and growth hormones
Seeping into the ground   flowing underground   northerly
Up through the aquifer's
Veins   into the wells   through everyone's bodies

Thrift stores   to spend the few dollars
Left over after utilities
And the requisite bag of pintos
The sack of flour for tortillas
A bucket of dried corn
To grind

O   a couch and soft chairs
Sounding like the gospel refrain
When she says it out loud   *Ooooo*

To dream
Long and deep enough
Inside the purple warm throat of sleep

———

Quiet as a cave
The recent battle—a scrap heap of festering
Her hope—they never return
Run out of gas
Lose a tire
Be found out

———

The border crossers from Mexico working in her garden
For a plate of beans rice and a tortilla with lemonade say
Su hijo habla con las plantas en el jardín pero no con personas
Fíjese señora que se parece que las plantas responden a él también

She only caught some of the words then they repeated them again
slower She filled in the blanks
(Translation: Ma'am your son talks to the plants in the garden
Not with people   go figure ma'am
Looks like the plants are answering him as well.)

He is like the birds. The plants need the bird songs or
They refuse to grow hardy.

The mound of rusted pipes
Wood headboards mashed by rot
Beetle-infested car tires
Glass panes shattered
Scattered by a fist of storm
Lizards blinking
From creases between wood cords
Their eyelids blistered by radioactive sun

All scream out   *Raven!*

In the future where everything bends
Going reverse and strains the lower
Back muscle of the universe
Where reverse and future are one and the same
Raven will rise   from the blueblack
Velvet backdrop of his wings

The bone pile has a voice and the voice of the bone pile
Says the soil by the bone pile
Is contaminated
Mother mother   water   the water   is spoiled
soil spoiled   spoiled   spoiled

She curses the graffiti on a table she wants
To hack with her hatchet

At the bone pile muscular yellow lizards
Only come out before sundown
Or just before dawn   pumping their chests
Up down up down
A peep show of push-ups for girl lizards   their form
Stamina
Scaly skin blushes lust-pink to crimson

The finite and infinite hem between   ego   desires   out of control

A candle on the house altar flickers
Coaxing *come near*
The Virgin's robes glittering rays of light
Like sharp golden arrows circling her womb
A puckering mouth where multiplying eggs spit forth
Like lava   her own breathing
In out
In   out
A heaving steadiness

Make this medicine

Pissing under a tree
A fast star flies across the sky   she
Walks to the stone sink   knows

Her earthen pot sits beneath a basin
A pot used for beans but finally broken
Used so much it finally gave up
One time too many beans too little water too much heat and
Too many years
Cracking open like a watermelon's rind engorges
Gives up and busts
Exploding with a *thhhuuhh ppsshhuh*
After too much   heat   water   and ripening

But because she was Indian poor
And knew about too much and too little
She glued it back
Because mostly everything is salvageable
When not thoroughly smashed

——

She felt the throbbing ache
Squats over the pot marked   *Not For Cooking*
Offering her warm blood each month
The first drops like chokecherry juice
Easing from sweet flesh on summer solstice

Learned from a master gardener named Bob
In the hills of Sonoma when a foundation in Santa Fe
Paid her and ten other Indians to see about
Learning his *Hippie-gone-real*
Biodynamic *method*

The Indians went for the trip
To get away from the rez a hot sun beans and tortillas
For one   week   in wine country

And when Bob served   organic salads   his best wine
They laughed in unison when he said
He figured out *how to squeeze mother earth's tits*
Hard enough to get milk

A thought Indians wouldn't voice   in front of whites
But Bob's wine was good
So they all laughed

Bob's lessons:
During *environmentally challenged* (the foundation's words)
Or
Fucked up times   (Bob's)
Soil needs teas from   the rain
Rocks   and   trees
Given back to her body

Feed the earth what she craves
The strongest medicine

Every month she offered
Minerals her body made
A twist on Bob's applied theory

An ApacheChicana midwife said
When women return to letting their blood flow
Back   onto   soil
Wars on earth   will   cease   but as long as men
and women
Shed   blood   of   death   on   her
Earth and people   will   perish

It was a story of stories older than this story
And made irrefutable sense

She figured she'd feed blood back
To the mother
Every month
And poured her tea onto the compost pile
On the moon's cycle

She'd only been on her moon for two days
And because it was cold weather
The teawater remained clear not moody
As it did very quickly in hotter months when
Monsoon   was   on   strongly

Tea the color of hibiscus
Glittering garnet geode
Fruit of the womb

Now the paintbrush a knife
A pot of hominy and beef tips
Cooking on the stove for dinner

She walks to the front shed   opens the padlock
Picks a natural bristle brush from a coffee can

Of long length and wide shape for painting pigments
On adobe walls in springtime
Dispelling old energy

———

Inside the warm round belly of the kitchen
She moves to the cabinet   pulls out a ceramic bowl
Mrs. Fiero the yard-sale lady gave her two summers ago
The hand-made bowl of lime-green slip on clay made in Mexico

"Mexican"
Indian women acknowledge
Brightness and color in the morning
No matter how treacherous and mechanized
Mexican   Indian   women   see
An impossible lightness and irrepressible dissent
in *chance*

———

She steadies her grip on the pot
Unhurriedly pours her blood tea into the bowl
Approving the juxtaposed colors
Cranberry of the fluid
Lime of the clay slip

Frida Kahlo comes to mind

Frida all in one stroke wanted to love and kill Diego
Bastard womanizer
Panzón she called him   Fatty Fat-man Fat-ass Fatso

Not as gifted as she
But larger and filling up more space

Frida knew she'd always have to let him   take that space
Because she'd fill it with him one way or another
Too little and too much
Whether he or she volunteered to be there or not

Her lips parted into a smile
Just like a new carnation
When the firm bud of skin
Begins to open its petals
All because someone kept watering and feeding the roots

———

She cradles the bowl like a mewing newborn
Takes the brush in her hand
Dips the tips of natural bristles   just a touch
Daubs the earth of the wall   a test patch
Gasps little puffs of breath   a low laugh
Because she is the only one listening

Painting the walls a blood-and-water fusion
Texturing across   back   across
Oohing and aahing as brown adobe washes red

Her naked hand in the red paint
Onto her face
Cool red fluid
Veining her   eyes   nose   mouth

———

How high do you have to hold a cup filled with liquid
For the liquid to ribbon and twirl like a rope
Was the only question left

And the swirling reminded her of DNA strands
Glossy with chance and timing
New lovers plummeting through the sky
Who climax just as one pulls
Her talons away before collision
Where everything that was ever created is
Spiraling from the cup into the simmering posole
Jewel fluid's stream blended into food
From beginning to end
Swelling hominy   beef tips
Churning wild sage   coriander
Fortifying the bodies

———

Over the pot of aromas steaming
A shielding shawl
She prayed
To the corn and beef tip grandmothers

———

Beginning and the end and a beginning   *may the way*
Be in peace
I ask you great motherbeauty   hear me   blood of the living womb
Blood of newness and beginnings
Be the way   to end this war   end wars

May all who eat this stew
My garden womb   resurrect lightness

Splitting darkness
Catching prisms of light
May the way be in peace

May justice quicken her pace

What She Knows

She walked outside and the eyes of night
Beheld her relieving herself under a mesquite
While she watched a fast star fly the sky
Chasing the sun
Only to fly backwards into a future light
Seeding the star's eroded heart

She knows she doesn't know why
The father's first children scorned hers so
And hated because hating is the world's prescription
Justifying pain   distrust   nothing else to do

Why the father thirsted for ruin
Luring the small ones over trip wires
Loathing he inspired in a pecking order architected
To bring him some company at the bottom of his ladder
He clung to not seeing it wasn't the only way to the stars
Not believing other ways existed
Beyond bondage to fears and failures

Becoming the slave he built reprisal like a shrine
Corrupting his sons and all his generations
Who trespassed a small girl's body

Raven   with   beauty   all   around   him
Grasped the unspeakable
And grasping on tightly to vestiges of what remained
In a world with little left for naming

Raven unfurled the tree inside his heart
Like the mesquite tree where his mother
Buried her miscarried young
Who never had a chance against DDT and poisoned wells

He'd watched her fold their bodies   down   down
Next to the tree's roots
His tree like hers rained tiny leaves and pollen
Of songbirds murmuring memory

The First Being She Saw Was the Tree

The damp air pastes a poultice on my face
Mesquite leaves veiling my hair
Tiny leaves scattered like stars

Today is cool
Everything is convinced
This is autumn

Mesquite   the wild amaranth   corn   and rye
All taken in by a spell
Unpredicted weather

Trees denude themselves
From the past
Bare their bones to the world's eyes

Who mostly see them dead   or ugly

Though the roots   allthewhile   thrust downward
Webbing through quarried aquifer
For food   strength   water

Last night I prayed for a lover
Staring at moonlight   seeing glow
A hazy dome over the city beyond

Wondered if I woke up in another land
A different woman   different life
If I'd still pray for a lover

Would my life be that different
Would I still yearn for the scent of hard rain
A lover's hands on my skin

My infant's short toes seeking warmth
Between my thighs
What do we do with second chances

Show our secret face
Sweet face   will you   kiss me   face
Know me   talk to me   hear me

Share me   show me face
Protest with me   clean up with me
Make a child with me

That face
In the next chance will I
Be the truth

Not avoid it
My children sprinkle seeds
Like flowers they hope me to be

Believe I can be
Pushing up earth's tilthy crust
Unfurl my small head   rise straight

Feeding on the scarce good and abundant toxic
My desires collected in the harvest by their small hands
My fervor to be loved   makes me an object   mere material

A paradox that sinks us
Separate this seed from its chaff
Skilled at separating

My children's fingers move like tendrils
Over the railing of adult words
Seeking to know us   our secrets

Wanting to be touched   with care
Be heard seen   welcomed
Raised as equals

Navigating through herbicidal clouds
Sometimes I feel
Contaminated through and through

Sometimes I feel
I am alive
It is a potion in my eyes

Love juice of new visions
Bursts of freshly picked flowers
My imagined wholeness

A healing
The children's whole selves singing
Knowing possibilities

The wonderful mess   without fear

The shadow across the room
Matures ugly and large
To the will of the collective

Blanketed by mesquite pollen and leaves
I came awake and saw the tree
Who speaks more truths than humans

I am getting away with nothing at all
Surely a spirit stands in my defense
Or one of my children said a prayer for me

Mr. Fear forgot to sink
His little splinters in my feet
I woke up feeling   briefly

I was breeze

Corn Girl

Breaths taken slowly   filling capillaries

More blood circulating   actions to other actions

My breaths
Spread   blend   becoming and dissolving
All I can think is
What is always at stake—losing you

Back to breath

In   all that is unforgotten
Out all that is necessary

Go forward

———

I ask about forgiveness
As if I could
As if I had a right to

Your fingers
Ripple forward on the flute

You take a breath
Forward again   breath

Steady steady
Quick then slow

Feel   breath move you
Slowing you   as breath

Moves out

You clamp down

Our wreckage
All around

Raven

In dreams his mother paints a tree onto her face

Lays down   lays down   lays down the blood

And the tree is bleeding
The tree and the blood overtake her
Until she is only red

——

He is conscious   alone in the hot dirt

In the forest of his heart

Sprouts evolve   into stems   branches

Overtaken by the trees

——

Ravens are the most intelligent of all birds

Their brains carry early stages of
What we   recall   a radiance   moment in time   Revolution

Moving fast
Across the sky

Raven pulled the lottery ticket
To catch the first humans from a wild rose constellation

And shape them into muscle and blood
But Raven smart as he is
Couldn't help looking at the fish-scale shimmer-glitter
Stars   and when he wrecked   he broke through the
Thinning shell
Into mischief   misterchief   a chief   wandering without
A name or tribe or band or soul   or clan
And when Raven blinked back
Into this wreck of a world
It was too little and too late
Mischief harvested and mined his own sons
Teaching them to peck their order
With little left for naming

———

Inside his body that won't fight back
Huddling over
A sting to the back of his head
Fist at the nape of his neck
A body   sitting on his   pins him   down down   all the
Way down

Two hands grip Raven's head
And pound his skull into hot dirt
Brittle tumbleweed   stickers
Dirt and stickers cake with drool
Oozing from his mouth

Raven
Who knows about lies, destruction, and endings

Knows
Not to say any words

———

His mother paints a
Blood tree
Onto his face

O! Stars!
O! Grandmothers!
O! Tree!
O! Raven!

Nobody hears

Not the sound

Nor the thought

Thanks to the following supporters of this project:

Joni Adamson; Teresa Leal; Rachel Stein; Lori Riddle; Laura Tohe; Elizabeth McNeil; Patti Hartmann; Norman Dubie; Simon Ortiz; Arthur Vogelsang (APR), the first and one of the few U.S. editors who broke rank—for your encouragement and commitment to these voices; David Mitchell and the audience of the Tucson Poetry Crawl, summer 2005—for your irrepressible enthusiasm for poetry of witness from the shadows of the globalized, terrorized borders; Allison Hedge-Coke, who knows that poetry is not enough, it is only one tool—sister in war and in struggle, keep those loving e-mails coming my way; Elizabeth Woody; Heid Erdrich; Kim Blaeser; Debbie and all the staff at Antigone Books (Tucson, Arizona); Bob, Betsy, and the faithful at Book People (Moscow, Idaho); Susan Banes (Broad Perspectives talk show) and the supporters of KXCI in Tucson; Whitney Weirick, D'ana Soto; my mother, Eloisa Garcia Cavazos Tamez, and my father, in memoriam, Luis Carrasco Tamez, and all the relatives in Apachería (South Texas), confined in the barbed internment spaces between Calaboz, Premont, and Redford; Meg Gillo—a fine and careful reader; to my students at Pima Community College and The University of Arizona–South; Gina Franco and Meg Files—who both supported and trusted my teaching of witness, struggle, and refusal; Kristi Chester-Vance (for seeing); Ofelia Zepeda (for belief in this project); Nancy Arora (for the second time around); Kathryn Conrad and the marketing staff at the University of Arizona Press for on-going efforts to shift paradigms to the Indigenous and for trusting me; Anne Keyl, design editor, thank you for committing to an Indigenous artist for cover design and the positive economic impact that has on Indigenous people; finally, heartfelt gratitude to my dear friends, colleagues, and mentors at Washington State University, who listened patiently to me process and struggle in the final editing stages of this project to make what was invisible visible, and whose commitments to justice with regard to sexualized violence in Indigenous communities impacted this project—Jody Pepion, Ayano Ginoza, Christina Garcia, David Warner, Purba Das, Michelle Jack, Linda Heidenreich, Noel Sturgeon, Marian Sciachitano, Judy Meuth, and José Alamillo. All my relations.

About the Author

Margo Tamez's publications include *Naked Wanting* (The University of Arizona Press 2003); a chapbook, *Alleys & Allies* (Saddle Tramp Press 1991); and a collection of creative nonfiction, *The Daughter of Lightning* (Kore Press 2007). She is of Lipan and Jumano Apache and Spanish Land Grant ancestry of South Texas. She is a GRACe Scholar in the American Studies doctoral program at Washington State University and currently lives in Pullman, Washington.